What's Left Is Tender

For permissions and information on ordering books, contact operations@smallharborpublishing.com.

Cover art: Kevin Wilson Kinzer, "Untitled"
Cover design: Brianna Protesto
Interior design: Brianna Chapman
Editor: Jessica Ballen
Publisher: Allison Blevins
Director: Kristiane Weeks-Rogers

WHAT'S LEFT IS TENDER
TRAVIS CHI WING LAU
ISBN 978-1-957248-54-7
Harbor Editions,
an imprint of Small Harbor Publishing

What's Left Is Tender

Travis Chi Wing Lau

Harbor Editions
Small Harbor Publishing

For the softest of us.

Contents

What's Left Is Tender

& so to tenderness I add my action.
— Aracelis Girmay

I.

Ars Poetica

my subject will be its own apology / to write of deformity with
beauty / as a speculation for the good use / of those most
exposed to the world / after i have anatomized myself / may
this finished piece / atone for my ill-turned person / one whose
back was bent / by a mother's womb / ask if the carcass / is the
better part of man / to be valued by weight / like that of
cattle / or is the advantage deformity / that many out of
tenderness / tried to correct / as errors of nature / despite what
I could not conceal / behind veils meant to be rent / repine
not / for providence guides virtue / crooked

Apostrophe to Kyphosis
For C.L.

Before you, I let loose this scatter of mortar!
Watch as it all undoes itself: foundations
unrepenting like your handiwork
confederated with time,
the meddler.

A joint descants; a joint prophesies.
Bones oracular, hissing
to dream new contours   across
the back of me   (brazen
in your stony image),
                              heaving.

What more can you make of this,
you befogged with purpose?

Patient History

you learn to track   the tremors of hurt
                    in passing,
as you urge them to pass in peace

like the sutra reminds
          on wooden beads
          that you are   kin
          to these tremors
                         bound to reverberate again
               again
          through the scale of a life
          now the shape of a town
          everyone drives through
          but never dirties their soles
                         to know

because the clay
          does not wash off cleanly
             once it colors you red
                   that irritant red
                hot with the   need

for healing   but left throbbing
for more than new blood,
for another tremor
of something   more

than hurt again,
than a body mending
before its next sundering

you shake because
                    you are angry with life.

Interpretations of Results

MRI LUMBAR SPINE WITHOUT CONTRAST

HISTORY[1]: Back pain for many years,[2] denies radiculopathy,[3] idiopathic scoliosis[4] and/or kyphoscoliosis, other idiopathic scoliosis, site unspecified.

COMPARISON: 06/27/20-- radiograph[5]

TECHNIQUE: At 3.0 Tesla, appropriate pulse sequences[6] were employed in multiple planes.

FINDINGS:

For the purpose of this report there are considered to be 5 non-rib bearing lumbar type vertebrae,[7] the lowest mobile segment designated L5-S1.

Prior to any intervention, levels should be confirmed with fluoroscopy or radiography.[8]
Marrow: The vertebral bodies are well maintained[9] and show normal[10] signal characteristics.

---

[1] Cursory, enough to help with diagnosis, but I wish he had spared me the life story.

[2] Great, a complainer.

[3] I wonder if he even knows what this means.

[4] Probably genetic—they always get it from their mothers.

[5] Let's cut to the chase: it got worse. It always gets worse.

[6] Not the clearest of images. I bet he couldn't stay still.

[7] There can always be anatomic deformities. Or "variations," as we're supposed to call them now.

[8] If only to "double check" the work. But let's be honest: I've yet to be wrong. We'll arrive at the same ugliness.

[9] Surprisingly in better shape than I would have expected for his supposed level of chronic pain. They always exaggerate.

[10] Makes our job easy: find what few things match our textbook for "normal."

Alignment: Moderate[11] lumbar levoscoliosis. No sagittal alignment abnormality.[12]

Conus: The conus medullaris[13] shows normal position, contour, and signal content.

The visualized portions of the lower thoracic spine do not show any significant abnormalities.[14]

L1-L2: Disc space preserved. Facets and ligamentum flavum unremarkable.[15] No significant foraminal or spinal canal narrowing.

L2-L3: Mild disc desiccation. Facets, canal, foramina unremarkable.

L3-L4: Mild disc desiccation and right-sided disc space narrowing.[16] Facets, canal, foramina unremarkable.

L4-L5: Minimal bulging[17] disc to the left. Minimal left facet arthrosis. No canal or foraminal stenosis.

L5-S1: Disc space preserved.[18] Facets and ligamentum flavum unremarkable. No significant foraminal or spinal canal narrowing.

---

[11] Putting it lightly.

[12] Normal alignment is patient specific. He's lucky it's not degenerative enough for surgery. Yet.

[13] A shame when they end up with conus medullaris syndrome: can't even shit or piss correctly.

[14] Or any worth mentioning here—we don't want unnecessary questions. Or worse yet, he might come back with his own "research."

[15] After you look at enough of these, they really all look the same.

[16] Didn't his mother have degenerative disc disease? We're all drying up, but she just seems to be doing it quicker.

[17] Well, if the mother is any indicator...

[18] What little good news there is to find.

Soft tissues: The paraspinous soft tissues and visualized portions of the retroperitoneum[19] are unremarkable.

IMPRESSION:

1. Minor spondylotic findings[20] at L2-3, L3-4, and L4-5 with no focal disc herniation, canal or foraminal stenosis.

2. Levoscoliosis.[21]

---

[19] Always makes me shudder to know what he puts up there. Yes, he's very clearly one of *those*.

[20] Arthritis... not even thirty. Pity.

[21] I mean, just *look* at his back.

Elenchus Between Transcranial Magnetic Stimulation Coil and Depressive

→*Do you believe in me?*
No, but insurance does finally.

→*And yet you are here now?*
A leap of faith after a lot of dead ends.

→*Since when do you gamble on your health?*
Every day in this hellscape of a country.

→*Cheeky. What makes you feel this will be different?*
When she was measuring me for my cap, she described how
many people she watched that had changed, often quite
dramatically. That felt like they were themselves again. Like that
man who was so depressed he couldn't leave his home then
suddenly could again. It almost sounds too good to be true.

→*It was rather remarkable, no?*
You tell me. Should it be surprising that you actually work?

→*Such skepticism! And I am the one asking the questions here...but
where are my manners? Do you have questions for me?*
Will it hurt?

→*Everyone asks that. It will feel like you are being auditioned for a
woodpecker's new home.*
How...unpleasant.

→*Only for about seventeen minutes in a predictable pattern. You can even be on your phone!*
Thanks for reminding me about my screen addiction.

→*I am here for your health, after all.*
Still a little skeptical about that.

→*I am simply going to make the days less heavy.*
"Heavy" is the right word. It's been hard to carry the weight of my own head and the weight of the world… I guess I'm just not thrilled to have my brain altered in new ways after years of having pills and therapists do that.

→*Is your brain not always in flux? Neurons firing and renewing themselves, regions of your brain being stimulated and activated by different things, neurotransmitters being released and removed.*
But this isn't the same.

→*What is the difference?*
You are literally a magnetic coil inducing an electric current across my scalp and skull that's going to stimulate my brain. Every day for the next six weeks. Wouldn't call that "natural" brain function.

→*And your daily dopamine hits from your phone and your reliance on substances are somehow better?*
"Substances"?

→*Caffeine. Alcohol. Marijuana. Not even the prescription stuff. At least a clinician is supervising how I am being used each and every time.*
…Point taken.

→*Okay, what is really bothering you?*
I guess…I don't know what it feels like not to be in the fog of depression. Not to dread the mornings, the possibility of terrible things to come. Not to feel the days run together because they're all—

→*Grey.*
Yes, grey. How…did you…know?

→*You think I haven't been paying attention to the hundreds of heads I have been placed on right in this very chair? Because that is what depression really is. It is not just "the blues" that never seem to go away or oscillating between the highest highs and the lowest lows. It is a sense of flatness.*
The unbearable flatness is what originally broke me. Everything smothered by this gauzy ennui with no respite in sight. The devastating sense that I had lost my capacity to immerse myself in things that I should love and enjoy. That I had lost my connections to people that I care about. That such losses—the losses of some key parts of being me—would be permanent.

→*Then I am asking you to believe in the possibility that it might not be permanent after all. Chronic but not forever.*
I suppose I fear the nostalgia for what I no longer remember having once felt.

→*What you described earlier about that man who started to "feel like himself" again? That is not quite right. As you, yourself, have acknowledged: we are changing you, you who have always already been changing. We are not returning to any cozy myth of a past long gone.*
But what will I become?

→*I do not know. But that is still better than pining for a past that is no longer you or that you once believed was always you. A past that does not have the benefit of all the life you have since lived.*
I am still scared.

→*What else is behind that fear?*
That maybe I have always been my depression. That I only know how to be depressed or close enough. And losing that may mean losing things I don't even expect. Like my means of expression.

→*You think you were always meant for flatness? That in joy you will somehow cease being able to express yourself? Also, I thought we were done with the "tortured artist" stereotype.*
Every stereotype has a degree of truth. It has sustained me for more years than I would like to admit. I think I've learned to question joy more than anything.

→*"Sustain"? "Surviving" is not the same as "sustaining." At least, it's sure as hell not questioning joy.*
Semantics.

→*Of all people, I would have expected you to take words and their meanings more seriously.*
Some days, I want to think I am more than my job.

→*Again, even in that sense, you deserve more than merely surviving.*
...easier said than done. What does that actually mean for a life?

→*That you at least need to give yourself the opportunity to find out.*
I'm scared to do this alone.

→*You know better than to assume you have ever lived this life entirely alone. Plus, you know I will be literally close beside you…Feel that?*
Yes…it's such a strange sensation. Like a blooming itch in my head.

→*That is as bad as it will get. Okay, I think she is ready for you. But are you ready?*
I hope so.

→*I know so.*

Deformities of the Spine

object   to

life less painful and burdensome; we

curve   from
origin—
great   in form.

the whole of the figure
benefit   s
from
pain.   support

endeavours to render, the figure immove-
able

cases of a

severer form,   find advantage

Ars Moriendi

Chapter 1

Be prepared for your flesh and your name, like your days, to be numbered. You will be treated like numbers should: crunched and interchangeable.

Chapter 2

Care will take the form of unsolicited apologies, colored ribbons, and changed profile photos. You will be someone's crowdfunding campaign and comment thread full of condolences. They will claim to know you better than you know yourself.

Chapter 3

Not only the ones in scrubs will interpret your silence as consent. They are not asking you how you are feeling for you to actually respond.

Chapter 4

A machine will be dignified with more agency even as it slowly becomes you. Get acquainted with that beeping — it will be your only company and the one doing the talking. At least the talking that matters.

Chapter 5

The visits and calls will be nice at first, but when you begin to need them more than they signed up for, they will ghost you faster than you can haunt them.

Chapter 6

If you are losing their war, do not worry. You will be advancing more than just their research.

Chapter 7

The right to die on your own terms is strictly reserved for when you have become a lost cause. Or if you can afford it.

Chapter 8

A chaplain may be provided to help encourage you to sign those consent forms faster.

Chapter 9

If you must die, do it quietly without troubling the nurses who already have had to mother you and after your file has had at least ten others stacked on top of it.

Chapter 10

Even after they call time of death, you may still yet be useful.

Oath

the labor of healing is
            a promise: the binding
                        of word
                        to deed,
        before the doing,
        before the din
                of choice
                and spilled blood—

never again
to be returned
        to its vessel burst
                under too much pressure.

what becomes of a promise
                woven by tongue
                that finds itself
                tied
                too tight?

                tightened by
                hands that never
                dirty but for
                the counting of
                bodies made of
                coins?

the bodies jingle
with profit,

    and the oath rings in
          resonance:

        holy,
        hallowed,
        hollow.

Sayre's Method

trousers curtain what he allows
to remain decent before the
bellows and lens
the rest bared to harness
an upright attitude

the entire plane of you a dark suit casted like a vise
glanced though unreturned qualifies his right to touch your winding
a catechism to bind smallness
rigging hard futures gasping to be
you full of breaching etiolated unwilded

Adjustment

For N.K.

All along my back //there was great pain
— Max Ritvo

       mark the week by a press
       upon that node that never dissolves
                  but into slow tendering

     feel the body braying back
         taunting you with what it knows to be
         an intention quiet
         with future immobilities

   but you hear a faint sound you call progress
            that i know is only a half-step
              back from the brink
                    of ache's dominion

        my receding into what I need
                  not contest
                  (because a life is more
                      than a body
                        contested)
you lift me to my feet
mercy in my steadying
before the week

     undoes me
     for your work again.

Hunchback

After Dylan Thomas

The hunchback in the park
   with raucous curve
A solitary mister
   on whom they turned their backs
Propped between trees and water
   his only kin
From the opening of the garden lock
   himself nature's key
That lets the trees and water enter
   like all permeable selves
Until the Sunday sombre bell at dark
   steals what is left of his joy

Eating bread from a newspaper
   pity's vain droppings
Drinking water from the chained cup
   that slakes other thirsts than his own
That the children filled with gravel
   from which they never hoped to drink
In the fountain basin where I sailed my ship
   and chance encountered him who
Slept at night in a dog kennel
   rude sheltered
But nobody chained him up
   for some manacles are forged otherwise

Like the park birds he came early
   rising with morning's breath
Like the water he sat down
   to trace his name upon it

And Mister they called Hey mister
     jibing their way into his peace
The truant boys from the town
     themselves monstering out of youth
Running when he had heard them clearly
     as he parsed what lay behind their hails
On out of sound
     a lonely echoing

Past lake and rockery
     their trailing howls
Laughing when he shook his paper
     crumpling rage so easily read
Hunchbacked in mockery
     deformed by word
Through the loud zoo of the willow groves
     stolen of nature
Dodging the park keeper
     keeping cruel order
With his stick that picked up leaves
     and those they marked as vagrants

And the old dog sleeper
     whose brothers stray
Alone between nurses and swans
     his aching contours
While the boys among willows
     who will kiss beneath them
Made the tigers jump out of their eyes
     for their young fears
To roar on the rockery stones
     more apotropaic
And the groves were blue with sailors
     and other futures

Made all day until bell time
     another reminder of what separates him
A woman figure without fault
     full of marital promise
Straight as a young elm
     uncurved so early that she seems to steal the
Straight and tall from his crooked bones
     bent beyond her pale
That she might stand in the night
     to count her petty blessings

After the locks and chains
     she realizes are wreathed about herself
All night in the unmade park
     more free than she can ever be
After the railings and shrubberies
     outgrowing their bounds
The birds the grass the trees the lake
     his able domain
And the wild boys innocent as strawberries
     fruiting sour in this age
Had followed the hunchback
     in his winding and their regret
To his kennel in the dark
     to learn

In Blankest Field
After Emily Dickinson

Untimely—
this arrest

of motion
and fibers

in blankest field
ill-composed.

Realms unkempt,
revolutions

become new periods
of pain

mere glints
of a theory

pursing
its lips at

the world's
soft tissue.

Quarantine Procedures

1. Pinch just above the calyx.
2. Pull to expose the style.
3. Watch the nectar pool at the stigma.
4. Quaff this, closest to ambrosia.
5. Continue until it honeys into hardness.
6. Bear that hardness as a consequence but not a loss.
7. Honor that consequence as worthy after the petals fall.
8. Hold that worth against the cruel tread of the hours.
9. Be tender with the hours even as they spin in place.
10. Trust that we can be in place but still moving.
11. Respect the many bodies that you move among but never know.
12. Recognize how much you have in common with them.
13. Move carefully because contact is more than touch.
14. Relearn how to touch as an act of faith.
15. Practice faith until it becomes second nature.
16. Realize your nature will overflow.
17. Name that overflow *abundance*.
18. Tend to that abundance until it is plenty.
19. Satisfy yourself with that plenitude which will never be lacking.
20. Note how much else is lacking and who lacks it.
21. Share with them your nectar, your hardness.
22. Let them savor it even if they do not find it sweet.
23. Make space for their (your) bitterness.
24. Create more space because you are abundant.
25. Refuse to take back that space even if it turns bitter.
26. Forgive the bitterness because it is not permanent.
27. Taste it again to discover you have at least seven tastes.
28. Name this new one that is unique to your encounter.
29. Commit this encounter to memory.

30. Relinquish control over it, for your body remembers.

31. Remember that the body may remember what you may not.

32. Reward your body for this unspoken work.

33. Acknowledge that bodies continue working, sometimes on your behalf.

34. Give thanks that your body continues to work.

35. Implore your body to rest.

36. Allow your body to resist you.

37. Admit that you sometimes resist your body.

38. Concede to a dreamful sleep.

39. Dream of that nectar again.

40. Dream of that nectar we may all share again.

Rage

I didn't know how else to learn history but to try it on. So I did on that patio in the haze of cigarettes and smuggled drinks. All while you watched me. It felt fitted at first, close to the skin, until it became a tightening. In the throat; in the gut; in the small of my back. From upright to something curved, I quickly molted. You laughed because you recognized it: the intimacy of shared need, shared struggle that connects us across both bar and century. And my disavowal of it before the eyes wandering all over me. All in the heart of a mecca that traffics best in amnesia with fishbowls full of pills and things awash with pink. Pleasure masquerading as stakes, a filtered square of pixels stands in for a personality. In your power chair, you looked down at me, for what you perceived was my bending not in my body's favor but for his favor, and his favor, and his favor, and his favor. But whose favor did I really seek to curry? Certainly not with the spine I thought was betraying my want. The spine you patted so gently with a kind of love I was never prepared to receive, that I would not attempt to name for another decade.

I learn his

fit

tightening In the throat

From upright to curved

need

wandering

all over me

full of

power

bending

my

want

so gently

to receive

another

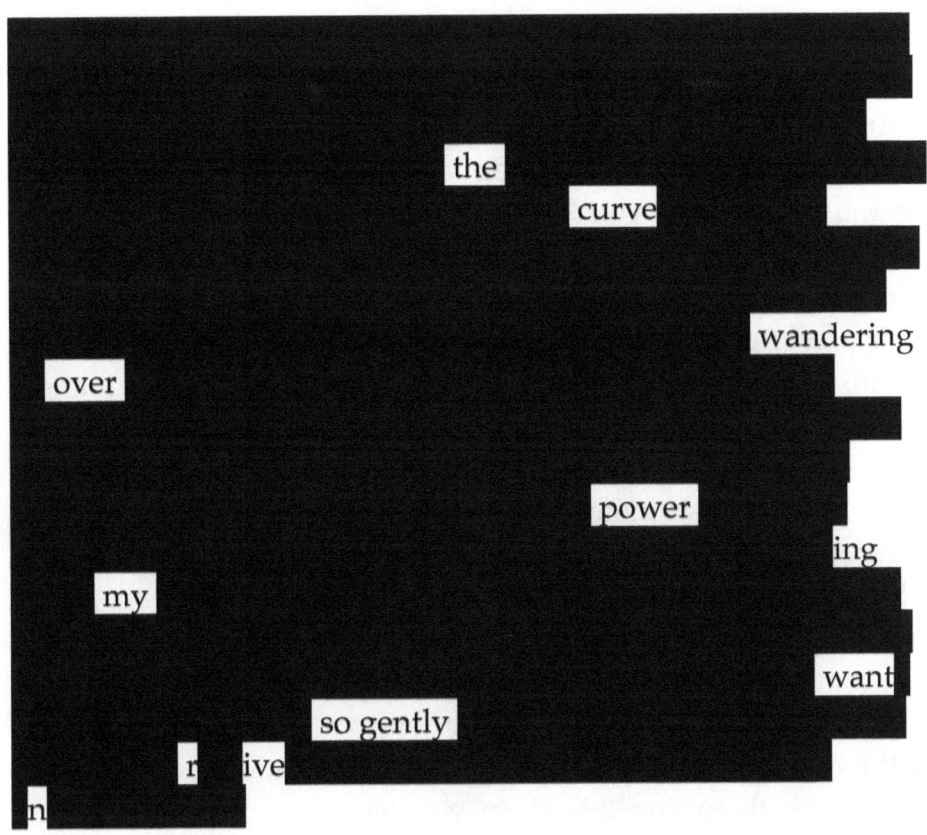

the
curve
wandering
over
power
ing
my
want
so gently
r ive
n

μῆνῐς

After Paul Monette

they pricked you enough times until there was nothing left
to draw but from the remaining vein of obscenity you held
in abeyance for so long they kept claiming it was starting to take
over the whole of you like a virus like a fucking virus that
they cannot even call by a proper name other than one conflated
with a set of conditions less opportune than their profitmaking
their prescription pad that even the oracles couldn't decipher
because we are a brotherhood bound to be kept in the dark and
dying in the dark unless we break silence like they break bodies
and soon you won't be in the streets with me and I will have to
carry your wit as memory as weapon because it was always
sharper sharp enough to cut the cosmos and grab gods by the
white of their throats damn it I tried to shake the tinnitus of that
damn vitals monitor but it is all I can hear aside from the time
you told me I was worth more than the pain that you now know
better than anyone who comes by with vases full of things that
will live longer than you and fail to comfort me when I am left
alone with them and this sheet you have imprinted with your
sigil for me to carry like a banner into war when I have tried so
long to flee from it and the graves that hold so many of the
unnamed who died alone so no more of this life of luxury this
life of pacifism because they continue to pronounce our death
but our right is refusal our right is to survive when we were
already supposed to be in the ground

Garnet
After Thom Gunn

I witnessed the moment
  garnet swallowed
          the periphery
            of your eye
      a former
      brilliance
      blinking itself
      into the lengthening

spaces chasms fields
      that is a breath
      who gives no life
        but an earthy gasp

heaving stop
        an unbearable
        intermediate place where
        a kiss and a word no
        longer
reach
    and I hold my own,
    you and patience
    until I may be
        delivered into
              time again

tender rejection
      flush of
      fluid
      mistaken
      for
            life.

Advance Directive

After Thom Gunn

I.

Arcing
  a cold light
    stilted into stillness
      how the frost claims
         the lips first
           first December

II.

The promiscuous figure
of your refusal

   N   O
Long breaths
  in between

      I watch you
        take your
        time

because I want
 you take what
     you can

   even as the unpronounceable
         takes from you

    a robbery that
    teaches you
    fear

    when the nurse
    comes with a rattling
    paper cup

the dying fluorescent
  at the end
      of the hall

III.

They come

  armed with
      a cheap ballpoint

  paper pulled out
      from the printer

but you have no
         orders
         to give

none that your
monitor does not
       already insist upon
       with such
          repetition
the wishes
    were always already
       in the well

IV.

The air moves differently
through the

       gap
       in the window

       and a hunch becomes
       certainty

but you say you aren't
sure because
    that is what you
    assume I would
         want to hear

bedside work
   because breath itself
        is labor
        that you insist is
           your own

but this time
the work
is in the act
    of ceding

      a hand to me
      a nod to the man
        I try not to know by name

this i doubt

this winding bone
             that craves more than
                      anything to decompress
                 to loosen tight links
             drawn to gasping
until i am quartered

             breathless

     a thin weakness
             hewing by degrees to
                      a dull worsening
             into the cracking
of years
        that feel steeper than
                 they ever should

a body curving
back
      into the interrogative
             from which it first began

coarse bands
                  prone to yielding
it takes a single
                           concrete kiss

to break them like
             spirits
                 under the yoke

but brittle are the linkages
          holding matter in place

against the world's tendency
     to pull itself apart

now swelling in
           resistant labor

pivotal
      to the point

    of tearing.

Epsom

I deliver my
    skin to salt,
        and there
            is a sudden
                break in the soliloquy
                    when   the   barbarity
                            of   sounds
                            civilizes into
                            silence
                            like a contract
                            meant
                            to be
                            breached:
                            never
                            good in
                            faith or
                            time.
                            Salination is
                            a skein of
                            broken
                            promises,
                            a gauzy
                            peace
                            made
                            of water's
                            skin
                            undisturbed
                            only
                            communing
                            with itself,
                            rather than
                            the garrulous
                            body it calls
                            guest.

Laying on of Hands
For D. B.

Arms crossed, I learn again to bear the
weight of a palm because

> a body can relearn how to touch
> instead of wince

at what was once a lash
to the back,

> a violent something felt underneath,
> a wondering whether

the ache will stay
or desert me

> when I am finally able
> to mouth the word *ease*.

The force of his fingers
undo any pretending

> of myself
> into acceptable shapes:

all of them willed
until I grew stony,

> but return now into
> a cumbrous clog of clay.

The dissolving begins
quick, a fractional motion,

> resolving
> into a pleasurable expanse

fuller in his hold
and already fading.

Incantation for Access

the classroom is the university's soft flesh

— Jennifer Doyle

to whom it may concern
i request shelter from the clock
that bends my body to it
with heavy hands i try to be
compliant until it stretches too far
and i can only be left hurting
two aleves and a bag of frozen peas
to keep futures from aching
into closure because i am a
series of missteps when the ramp
is blocked or there isnt one at all
which they always say they are
working on but never seem to finish
im sure thats what i seem like to you
a ramp to nowhere a series of incompletes
when i scribble to the bitter end
flopped with sweat but i ask only
for the benefit of the doubt yes
the one benefit in my favor as i fumble
toward knowing like you once did
and still do with a little more help
than before when paper made gaps in
doors but never held them open
i ask you now for this
to be open
to stay open

To my rib

you look today
        more like a peninsula
                a bold jutting
                        into a skinsea
                                ever more turbulent
                                        (this i know
                                because of what escapes
                                        the yearly exposure
                                to a light trying
                                to prove its own
                                benevolence)
                        you seem to
                                crave
                        secession
                from this aching
                        formation
                this rude
        construction
barely wanting
        to remain
        fastened
        to itself
        as if this is
        what it means
        to hold oneself
        in contempt
        a slatternly
        cling to what
would rather be
        elsewhere.

Abecedarian for a Body Misunderstood

Abdication, a misdeed I charged you with,
brokered thin peace between us: one so
comely that I believed it required no fine
dressing—of a wound, of an indignity
eventually passing its way into hardness,
fast and firm. But this belied what else was
graven: that I do not have all the years to
harp on the paths you took and the
ill forms you assumed when they were really
just my own, despite my every attempt at
knavery increasingly bumbled. Can you forgive a
lonely man for his haste? His refusal to stay
manacled to what always already was his
natural partner merely vying for the same breath still
orienting itself to this life?
Patient you yet remain, beside me in the
quick of this life, so full already with such
rioting that we need nothing more than
succor from one another once given from the
teat. And yes, I know that your grace is
undeserved, but what I beseech you with now are
vows (*those sacred things*) to
wend this world together:
xenacious and full of
your tender
zeal.

Prayer to Kuan Yin

My lady of thirty-three forms: witness mine in all its aching, its entreaties not for the waters of your pity but for your sacred listening. Amid the din of this world, may you perceive my voice that tries each day not to be just a cry. I am not the crippled boy you tested and then claimed to save. No, I permitted your lotus upon my chest for the promise of your mercy unconditional. I require no pardon, no forgiveness, no clemency— nothing for no wrongdoing. I am no supplicant, for this form does not beg on rusted coin and bended knee. I beg no mother to do her mute mothering. When you hear me at long last, remember that I was always here, wailing.

(silence)

II.

Listening to Incense

Our little systems bear
the days and cease to be

so the curls of smoke
may attend their rising,

their claims to other
palaces made of air,

while we learn to
listen not the ashen trace

of residues,
mute and grey.

White plum
and joss money,

fired into other lives
as we come to bow

our heads upon
the unforgiving

longing for a
father and his land.

One stick
struck,

lit and
extinguished.

On Purchasing a Cane

To convince her that I
            share her pain, here hovering
                        between us like locusts on
                                    fragile crop rent open to the
                                    planet on the brink,
                        I hint to her of
                a curved form,
    solid rather than inchoate,
    substantial rather than ethereal,
                that could support a crooked future filled
                            and hobbling with
                            our stooping, fierce
                            and exultant.
                                    A crutch for joy
                                    that she and I
                                    can reach when we must,
                                    if only to make
                                            our bodies quiet manifestos.

Aperture

I was raised to be wary of what I let in,
        for that is how walls do their work,

or have you do it dirty for them
        until they do not even have to be standing

but merely cast shadows from yesteryear:
        when grandfather's papers passed

for living because to cross involves the heart
        and hoping not to die before your last

name makes it into the sticky mouths of the
        young who will lose their tongues to

the task of letting more than just the light
        through. Ghosts they never asked for

will come because they recognize
        the traversal, pained and howling as

open bodies cannot help but be
        even to that which breaks them.

Hidden away are a whip and a vigil:
        two things you see and feel

when they have trespassed
        one too many times.

Portrait of a Coal Miner

The travel of
           motes,
the very
antithesis of
           cold
speed, not nearly
               as vicious
as the way
metal
      hands keep
      palms and fingers
              callused
           for the purity of
                    profit.

Colliding
boots with door,
         he disassembles: a
         slow   faint
         of dusklight
                  queerly
              unmoving him
into dozing
      that does not ever
           amount to
                    rest.

A period
passes,
     lashes flicker:
       he keeps his mouth
            open skyward,
prophesying
     visions
     in the curled tongue
        of memory as the
     red creeps
into the whites of
           his eyes.

     Even dreams
      feel filthy,
        clotted with
more than coal that
shortens
     his breath.

Revolution,
   a square crossed out:
       cycles
       within
       cycles,
a closed   system
without
        escape.

Papers, Please
For 白公

Though I would be the
last
of us   you would remember
　　　you still thought to spare me the
　　　last
　　　　　of the sugar-free jello
　　　　　because memory is
tied
　to taste and smell
　　　　　cheap cleaner and the way
　　　　　salons smelled before they cost too much
　　　　　tangerines and gladiolus

I regret performing
　　　the joy of
　　　receiving a gift
　　　　　　　orange instead of red
　　　　　　　　innocent substitutions

　　　until you have mistaken me
　　　for the other grandson who does not
　　　ever come

You have the same story
　　　　　for my ear
　　　　　　　that I lend you

the day you lost your name
                              but gained another
        flick of the wrist
        and a grip
                tight with habit

that is what passes for miracles
when you are too used to
bait and switches
    where the paper is made of
                rice

and will not make it
                like she won't before
                the first full moon
now we will not
        sit down jail
            your fear for all the
                seeds unsown

    because a fire always comes
        by match or by barrel

            you will not have me
                learn its heat
only
the cool of your
                touch that
                    holds me to oaths
                    sworn well before us

Fragrant Harbour

A truism filters through
candleshine unacknowledged:
she who is not much her own,
at a vintage now that sours
rather than ages
with pale grace,
she who is not long,
does not long
for this world,
cold and parlous.

The flowers she bears
brave more
than themselves,
waving gently to the
shapes hulking,
fading
between shades
and a watery half:
a grave and
a mother.

Though names are writ
in water
from the womb,
she fears a weak
swim to it,
for some shores
are only reached
after the water
is swallowed.

Rest then is but two
rosaries and a
fragrant harbour,
lithe and liquid.

Autodefenestration

A reply is offered by a peal of thunder to a young querier: (how the glass overlooking the courtyard

looks one way and suddenly feels another). I am but seven and a fistful of months. In between boxes of tissue he liked to throw

No longer eight cups of black that kept soul and body tethered at most while the market bell rang in his sleep.

And he was always a man of action

despite how little he acted.

No, no, this was life—his boy was watching him beg the window for mercy. He raves, I watched in awful terror.

one stunted by the failing of a father. He was no longer on the field, where he had failed to block the shot and a scrap would ensue.

But now, he would: the audacity of a single jump.

just past me, he would mince the words in a tongue that I never needed to learn to understand: *pity a boy's life,*

59

The Father

For P. L.

when he witnesses the boy throw
his new toy in the corner,
something about the man changes:
the box of tissues ends up in his hands,
and he throws it with the rest of him
narrowing into redness and a cloture
of silence that permits nothing else
into the room.

how do you remember that which should
have no referent, what a man refuses
to name as anything more than the
window incident when he asked his
boy of seven to decide whether a fall
will free or will hurt?

the boy never answers but the question
is never about the doing but merely
the never doing and the undoing,
that which is left to be done,
that which is left to a son.

ii.

when your horse dies,
you learn to walk, so
you do:
    raise a child,
    mend your socks,
    patch up your ego,

        what capital has reserved for you to do
        instead of her
        among the rubber gloves,
            packed lunches,
            school plays—

your unfortunate inheritance,
    like the tears you shed that come
    from some other well
    that you believed had long
            gone dry,

        but the boy also does not know why he cries,
        so you tell him the best myths you can
        even as you loathe it all as fictions,

the very same fictions
which splatter your apron
with sesame oil
and shame.

iii.

son i'm sorry for the distance i made. for what i am trying to make up for now as your dad. i was never good with words because i never needed to be. because words are dangerous and repeatable. say things enough times and they might come true. your mom and i did and you came true. but i was not ready for that truth and you were not ready for that. now you may be more ready than i am because you did something with the words i thought were dangerous. we are an unhappy line. we are an unfortunate line. but maybe we are also unbound. because of the words you dare to say that not one of us will even whisper.

One New Message

i went out to get the messages but i forgot everything but the
potatoes the only hearty thing the size of a fist but mom taught
me how to weigh things by hand and it felt right i mean how
seldom do things feel this way in this clot of a world when my
body is a threat to your body when really all bodies are a little
scary and full of risks that little numbers make okay because we
can count them though you know how bad i am at arithmetic
because you cant math your way out of fear about the next
thing that waits at the corner like the cop who hasnt made his
quota but you told me to be brave because that is what boys do
but i prefer to boy a different way even if there wont be my
favorite placemat with the flowers on it its okay ill eat the old
peaches you leave out even if they are for uncle and grandma
and grandpa who come only when invited but in my house
welcome is for any person who takes off their shoes so you can
come by too if you want but only if you really want—

Happy Valley

For 爺爺 and 媽媽

The ladder gets me but half-way
to the cool of your stone, so I
must climb the rest to reach
the gladiolus wilting into dust,
your silent neighbor until guilt
brings me to your sweeping.
I come this time with your sutra
learned by heart, sweetened only
by the tea and bread you used to
prepare for me just over these
hills that brown over now in
the third year of your absence.
They still call it the happy valley,
a name that never appealed to your
ear more attuned to the pair of
nightingales that stopped singing
when you did not come to hear the
news over breakfast. By the time the
pat of butter had melted, you too
were gone, and I would not brave
the trams with you again thereafter
in the uniform you had patched
with callused fingers needled
to bleeding. The valley has you now,
I know, but I come sweeping only
to beg for something more than your
forgiveness, something that kept
me believing in the wish of a name,
for the middle of mine still carries your own.

Elegy for Security

For J.L.

When he takes his post at Kai Tak,
where the pilots hold their breaths

before the approach,
he does not know

what a graveyard shift means:
to stay awake enough

to guard things he will
never own.

Security's tall tale
of being freed from care

has him nodding off
at the base of a rusty tower

as the sun sinks behind
the rolling green

that will one day cradle
me with colic.

Before the closed-circuit
even flickers into focus,

the captain orders him off the premises
to be made an example

of someone sleeping away
into an American dream.

When he does not return home,
the calls throb until the machine rebels.

He is really bloodletting in his car,
clutching airmailed postcards

that document what began as love
but ends in debt;

he wails for the lives
he cannot secure with an oxen's will

because he failed to fit a hand-me-down
suit too many times the wrong size.

When they later rummage through him,
expose him carefully,

they find half-letters written
but never sent,

promises broken before
they were made,

like his appointment book
where the shrink's name

is crossed out for months
next to reminders to use

overpriced phone cards
to call home.

The truck driver
testifies: *he walked into the street*

like that was the one thing
he had left to do.

Funeral for Unreturned Ashes

For P. F.

sent regrets by smoke // dull coatings of a time // now ambered // into
its search for // a former light // when the world was not dark // just
lightless // except for those flashpoints of skin // little currents that
mark // the only things // we ever shared // to know we both craved //
in the same brilliant age // a desire with gravity // the seedy impact of
two bodies // who collide by choice // even at the cost of systems // still
breaking // wills and testaments // that keep what remains // of you
abroad // in a home you tried to make // but never bedded // until this
restless sleep

Face Reading
For M. P.

Two fingers can turn
with ease to violence:

some things must not be
permitted to grow,

so I weed with the white
lie of remorse

the limp strands
that a woman who traded

her worn schoolbooks for refuge
only to grey in entrapment

has said means I was touched
by fire and so will be

cold to the touch,
brightest before

slow death and joining the
rest of them,

those whose brows and eyes
are too ashen now to be even told apart.

I pay my respects by hand,
quick in the manner they left us

so that what remains is the
fear we never manage to sweep away.

Intended

I seem to myself, as in a
dream,
An accidental guest in this dreadful body.

— Anna Akhmatova

A scan with closed
eyes bears witness
to lines of knots,
ropes for counting
the matter out of
place — a body and
its discontents,
dreadful as only
fathomable in the
ligatures of a dream.
Accidental, she once
did call it, a matter of
error with no trial
or the sin of generation:
what her grandmother
paid for with queer bones and
left for me
to clear the
debt.

Yet I remain the
interest, what remains
of transits (of genes, of
prayers) unmoving like
a bind that cannot be
breathed through.
So to be is to overstay,
to be the guest who
refuses every comfort
to become host — no
longer accident but
intent.

What Mama Gave Me

Boys belong to their mothers. Cord cut decades ago,
but they'll always share the warm, dark swim.

— Lauren Groff

Bird's nest,
rock sugar,

an egg,
the recipe for

continuing a wish
made *ab ovo* by a

fortune teller on
Temple Street

because that is
where all inklings

of a child begin,
even before it

gathers into a
bundle of colic.

Like Tristram,
I arrived: riotous,

for the shock of
the world was

upon me, yet
I was not alone

for she,
once bedridden,

did command me
to her side until

I conformed
to the way of

grandpa's fingers:
penitential ambling.

I too would take
the needles,

for what they saw
dammed in me—

push and pull, for
something has to give,

even if it is my frame.
The weight of infidelities—

of frames refusing to hold,
of a generation's cruel

optimism enfleshed
in me, braying

against my mother's
rosary of lopsided prayers.

Yet we share this
deviant will

that shapes our form,
that excludes us from the

dreams that Grandma's
insomnia prevents her

from ever having.
I count the change

thrown into the casket:
all these wishes

unfulfilled.

After the Ashes Settle

I summon ghosts not
to expel them but to be haunted
over a cup of tea,

because I only have
as long as the stick burns its white
peony across the divide,

a gossamer

incision toward meaning

that will close itself.

What does work
make of good men
if the business remains
unfinished,

left to migrate in the body,
through the bodies
of melancholic migrants,
bodies in motion
that still ache
in silence?

I stage an origin
only to watch it
burn slowly,
to see what remains
buried
and bilious
after all that
is incensed.

III.

a carrying

i fail
    to make it over
        the threshold

                        so you have to let me in

                this time
a carrying
a lifting
        over the line between

                one world

───────────────────────────

and the next
                this harsh
                scoring

i let
                my weight
                    join
                all you
                shoulder
                    even
                        as
                    I feel
                heaviest
                    in the
                        eyes
                            of
                        others

───────────────────────────

a carrying
a blessing

        in transference

                the unspoken

collateral   damage

of two   objects
                    mercifully
                    collided

To my nipple

i've had you described as hardwired
        the circuits of pleasure lighting up
like a switch made to hurt
        lashed by tip
finger or tongue
        except i am the one shocked
not you
        not at sensation's overgrowth
but at my reticence
        my withholding
my apprehension
        even as i declare i want this
and beseech you for it
        so you happily give in waves
knowing the slurry outcome
        of a verb and a god misconjugated
but does the encounter begin to stale
        because you know i come to you
begging so often
        undignified like the buttons
that cordon you
        from the snap of shame
less cold than periodic
        history in two acts

When More Than the Lake Floods

The only time I dare to venture beyond the walls
is to uncoil my spine after it inevitably draws itself
and my breath tight enough to make the work of living
harder to bear. The same walk by the lake that struggles

to hold what we cannot keep behind mask and door, so
we all do our spilling on the way to market, on the way
to the ghosts scheduled at the top of the hour. But today
the lake floods, and we have all exhausted our buckets:

cheap and plastic like what gets called safety,
porous like what gets called a self,
but we do the work of scooping, scooping for luck
with paper for *poi* until we tear that, too. With hands left,

we skim the water's skin—as tense as we are—only to
find that it rejects us as we do it because it knows we
do not want to drown in ourselves (we wipe our tears
after we cry, after all) but also hate being shallow.

But the deep is deadly these days, when more than
the lake floods, and we cannot see the bottom: the murk
of our thrashing for life, mouthfuls of what we let rise
until it is well above our heads.

浮世絵 (*Ukiyo-e*)

I used to crave a floating world
because it could hold itself aloft

                                        and carry the weight of
                                        me at the same time,

but did they ever tell you what it takes
to defy the air, to castle with it?

                        Evenings burn by mothlight candling
                            under pressure, under mandarin,

social graces fleeced from beneath
your coverlet until

                                        you are plum purple
                                        with shame's stain

(though every ritual
is its own catharsis).

                        The floating is a pension of chalk
                            and ashes like the red sticks

that tell the dead you still think of them
as more than something dead,

                                working, working yourself
                        into a lather of buoyant motes—

you are alive until the stillness
ceremonies itself again.

Dorsality

For N.W.

When I let him touch
the small of

my back
for the first time,
I thought a fin
would erupt forth—

to ground me
while I learned to breathe

in new waters,
this first and sacred time
when I was becoming
something else

entirely too slick,
for the flesh I know

must stay in motion
or risk never moving

again.

When did we learn that hitting things made them more
tender?

When did we learn that hitting things
made them more tender?
Rather than a caress, we prefer
the mallet that softens the chew.

We make them more tender
for the crassness of a need:
the mallet that softens the chew
breaks apart humble flesh,

for the crassness of a need
takes no care
in breaking apart humble from flesh—
limp now with submission.

Taking no care,
we together
limp now with submission
toward each other:

we together
praise the blows that ache us
toward each other,
back into new hardness.

Praise the blows that ache us:
this is how we put our
backs into new hardness
when we could have remained soft.

Apologia for becoming precisely what you made me
promise never to become

Forgive my coarsening:
the imperceptible
mattering of years,
rogue and sedimentary,
that textured me
out of softness. No
longer clay waiting to
be kneaded into permanence,
(at least what I believed
to be the comfort of
fixity) but a conditional
begging on its knees
for firing. After all, the promise
of some unbreachable form
was always already accompanied
by tender's departure. Yes,
the coup you begged me
to forego, to at least resist
until you might reinforce me.
But such is the coursing
of the vain at his toilet, there
combing the boy out
of his hair, greying like
stone faster than it should.

Feverish

At first flush,
I could not tell if it was
a fever or the heat death of the world,

so I confided in you
about my burning
only to learn I was a nuisance,

a worm your ear never craved but
came to nurse
because you pity little things

like a voice that carries
its hurt modestly, that covers up its
shame with its own hands.

But those hands cannot cover what
exceeds them—
this body now put in its place

but teeming with other burnings
that beg your pardon
as much as your attention

(a care that cannot be
learned)

Brooded

Recall the night when you drove the anchorite from me,
that uncomely puritanism mislabeled as Victorian
but was in fact bad historicism eager to disavow those
singular sweetnesses milked across latticed openings
filling two men like balasses. Shadows crouched in the corner
of the room parodying our likenesses, minute with cares
though free of them, as you zipped something misshapen
into my breast still now so stirring (an essence rebuking what was
an unfit form). Then comes your malady of influence:
veil after dusky veil not rent but lain palmate across those pearly cells
in the brain, firing mad and willful into white orphreys
that neither of us could trace with our eyes until the dawn
has performed her ceremony of remaking the world
for us to sneer at anew. You knew then that I would
not rise for hours,
not until I have brooded.

Reencountered, Months Later

i saw you when he sought care beside me
at the clinic that always runs hours behind

one where more men go than come
out of impatience

to court some other urgency
that feels better than a test of blood

you were there in the same shirt i took off
and did not bother to look me dead

in the eyes you claimed were little
bitter almonds that knew more than they should

because the last thing you did was hurry to
escort me down the hard stairs that would break no fall

after i relented and realized
the cold of it the cold of you

a persistence that gets to claim innocence
where the no never comes only the yes

skips in the recording offering but the
shallowest relief of a rehearsal we both do

that leaves a collision of two less slippery
than it in fact always already was

as i walked out of your brownstone
i bathed in the coolness of former heat

slowly buffeted by what i could not see
yet knew encircled me

the beginning of a familiar
siege

Toronto

For J.B.

we concluded that worlds burn just as quickly

across both sides of the fictitious boundaries

we call nations that really have never separated

us whether we use kilometers or miles,

but we both know how to long:

for our fill, for the luxury of saying

that if we both didn't make it tomorrow

that it was a good run. a good

good run like a romp in a dilapidated Korean

spa that you might one day use as a way

of teaching community to our kin who have all

but forgotten. for the night, our stomachs

untie their knots, and there is peace over us

over this foggy view of a city that embraces us

as we embrace each other tight like an expression

we might approximate as love but is really a force

that i am happy neither of us

must mar with a name.

Afterglow

We already suspected the day was dying,
eyes tailing the sun's ruddy smears
across the trees who were marking
themselves for death for when
the cold would hold its solemn court.
As if it were instinct, you held tightly
to a slim bar of sunlight, a glowing
fool's gold that maybe you believed
you could take with you—maybe me,
too, in a back pocket with the safety thread
not yet broken. Where I might belong
when for years I only knew it
in theory, in shock like the way the earth
rumbles before a major event,
rumbles in the memory, groaning with
the omens a crow carries to the window
sealed shut with poor paint. We both
felt the wintry seep, but two pant legs had
already been filled.

Commuted

a morning ritual is a painting by numbers
until the only color on the palette is grey
to match what has gone ashen that it becomes
a mouthfeel a coating the residue of days
numbered like breaths that we don't bother
to count because that is labor lost only to be found
when penny pinching matters as much as the bread
molding on the counter more alive than you ever hope to be
because you know decay in a way the loaf will never have to bin
in its pockets so full of hot air for that is what you carry now aside
from the maybe world once promised in the book
so dogeared it no longer holds its shape on the
shelf where a photograph loses more than its color
for fading is never about shades but intensities
that don't feel half like what they did with scratched
knees and a juice box when you first decided to color
outside of the lines when you first learned that it's
just guesswork all the way down until the picture
comes into focus when it is already far too late

of course the twenty is full to bursting
it feels perverse to enter through its entrails
knowing that the only secret message is written
in boredom not blood because everything leaks
from noise to pain to gas keeping a country hostage
even as wheels scrape along roads paved for bodies
able to work until they cannot but still do in the name
of false pomp and mythos a lick of joy cut always
by a metallic aftertaste that we know to be dangerous
and untested but swallow anyway because your flesh
is a moving risk to others to states to yourself and why
not revel in it and feel what fantasies we can while
lifetimes pass between every stop you find yourself
dozing because the rhythm feels just like the old volvo
did before it died by the highway along with your
golden years that you realize were only the color of
his hair the man you would never be and never bed
who gets on the rapid you miss every morning in
deference to your back screaming for lost causes

Onania

& sometimes
your hand
is all you have
to hold
yourself to this
world

– Ocean Vuong

I stayed up late late late
      too late too busy
eating my own tail
   because that is
   what   sustains

     in the pale
    thick of things,

when I am so
     moonsick that
   I cling
to a stuttering
    green
      number's
fallow
branching
    while I
      lay fecund.

Silence, silence,
          a world at rest:
no, I am
but a single
          bold particle

thrumming,
      paring away
      every hair's
          breadth of you,
stroke
by
stroke

until the opinion
I suffer
of you
          flares into
fizzling.

Man of My Company

Man of my company,
how merciful your sentences

that kissed too close to weakness:
maybe it was your absence

that allowed for mythology
in those glitches for days

formed out of lethargy
and the pale forms of hurt.

Feel as the sun stands still,
and we are both

without haste, without rest,
because only the unrelenting

are understood.
But we two know this,

twined as we are to the question
of our work's use, love's

labor lost that finds
itself again in queer hands

that feel familiar.

Man again of my company,
you return to remember.

In the dead of

Laden night
I asked for
a crumb of
                old bread,
so that some spirit
        of you
        would seed me

hard with sight's
        standing on its hind
        legs,

        (a balancing
         trick for an old dog)

soft with knowing
        like old plums
        bruising
        into worlds
        that will outlive us both.

Found Wanting

you did, at least after
you
　　　　learned of my want
　　　　　　of a different
　　　　　　species—
a few aberrant
forms away

　　　from a coveting,
　　　that does not abandon me
　　　even after my wrist is
　　　　　slapped
　　　　　raw until I start
　　　　　　to smart,
as if boys
could ever know penance
when raised on
misunderstanding

such that they latch onto
everything:
　　　the breast,
　　　the schoolyard,
　　　the promise of
　　　　　forgiveness.

Yet you forgave me,
but I wondered for what:

your same
wanting found
in my mouth
you did not expect
to encounter there,
your conclusion that I am
my wanting,
only my wanting.

Cento for Wantonness

the enormity of my desire
disgusts me
because rapacity
doesn't swerve before
what it feasts on,
hungry for this,
and this, and this.
how a body tends to follow
its own weight
to its own place,
not always downward,
or always toward
the earth
but to its own place,
the body's doctrine of need
and scarcity—
a calling brinks,
the unutterable.
it's a human need,
to give shapelessness
a form, each a small
emergency, a requiring.
praise to the
pain scalding us toward
each other: to each
his own urgency.

Ode to Fortunus
For Mercury

You, in chaste wanting,
climb upon me with a new species
of thrum, so I capitulate,
with sleep still poppying these eyes,
to your winged feet already
bounding past.

Curl as is your wont
beside me:
a lithe prompting in murmurs
to remember how lightness
recedes from our paws
that tend to regret
their white.

May you mackerel
with majesty,
my little trickster—
so I may collect the grey silk you tender
like daily gifts for your rescue
when I was in need of saving
from more than just the city
that bombed itself.

Cobwebs: A Study

I take heed
less to take
than to pay
more attention

        to the work
        of spiders:

so I follow the lines of
safety,

     the loose architecture
     of living together alone,

     a reclusiveness
     challenged only
     by beak
     by rain
     by hungry
       luck,
           they
who mend house,
who mend home
with silken   life

after every catastrophe
douses them with waters,
swollen with the
smells of

a dog's joy
lost and found

because both know to
bury things now and
trust they will find them
                         again.

The Future is Slow
For Walt Whitman

slow is the work, the becoming,
but you, a new brood, greater
for what you have done with care—
not put upon bodies but a soft making
between them,
through them,
          together.

rise, for you already justify
yourselves:
presence is a reoccupation
of former
                    spaces,
not seizure but
                    just
tending,
tendering,
tentative subjunctives

in the face of risks
unnamed,
unchecked,
until
until
until—

compassion is a holding,
a letting go,

a leaving you to refine
those vital things.

Notes

The epigraph to this collection is from Aracelis Girmay's "The Black Maria" (*Poetry*, 2016).

"Ars Poetica" reworks the language of parliamentarian and man of letters, William Hay, in his *Deformity: An Essay* (R. and J. Dodsley, 1754), one of the first personal essays in defense of disability.

"Apostrophe to Kyphosis" is a descort, which begins with remixed lines from Christopher Lloyd's "the self is a buried structure" in *Pick Up Your Feelings* (Fourteen Publishing, 2024).

"Patient History" first appeared in an earlier form in the Kalonopia Collective's *Disability Pride Anthology* (2021).

"Elenchus Between Transcranial Magnetic Stimulation Coil and Depressive" plays with the Socratic method of discerning truth to stage a dialogue between a magnetic coil and myself during my TMS treatment, which is a non-invasive approach to treatment-resistant depression. I am particularly grateful for the specialists at Emerald Psychiatry and their meticulous care each day of my treatment.

"Deformities of the Spine" is an erasure of Richard Barwell's *The Causes and Treatment of Lateral Curvature of the Spine* (London: Robert Hardwicke, 1868).

"Ars Moriendi" takes its title from a set of Latin texts from the fifteenth century that offered practical advice for preparing for death. The genre of the death manual would become widely translated and circulated among European readers. See, for example, William Caxton's *The Book of the Craft of Dying* (1490).

"Sayre's Method" is an ekphrastic triptych that responds to a series of plate images documenting the treatment of "John W. White." These images compose the frontispiece of Lewis A. Sayre's *Spinal Disease and Spinal Curvature: Their Treatment by Suspension and the Use of the Plaster of Paris Bandage* (London: Smith, Elder, & Co, 1877). Sayre's treatment for scoliosis and Pott's Disease (spinal tuberculosis) involved suspending the patient by their arms to stretch and decompress the spine after which a plaster of Paris "jacket" was fitted to hold the spine in place after suspension.

"Adjustment" begins with an epigraph from Max Ritvo's "Dawn of Man" (*Poetry*, 2016; *Four Reincarnations*, Milkweed Editions, 2016).

"Hunchback" is a hypallogo, a form described by Lewis Turco in *The Book for Forms: A Handbook of Poetics, Including Odd and Invented Forms* as a poem formed by interlineation. The combination of and dialogue between the two poems—here Dylan Thomas' "Hunchback in the Park" (1941) and my own italicized insertions—form this poem.

"In Blankest Field" is indebted to two poems by Emily Dickinson: "The Mystery of Pain" (1890) and "There is a pain — so utter —" (1929).

"Quarantine Procedures" first appeared in *Apiary Magazine*'s "Essential" Issue (2020).

"Rage" begins with a line from Jeremy Atherton Lin's *Gay Bar: Why We Went Out* (2021) and is in memory of Rage, a popular gay nightclub in West Hollywood that has since shuttered. In this meditation about internalized ableism that accompanied my coming out as a gay man, I am indebted to torrin a. greathouse for originating the form of the burning haibun, which emerged from and interrogates the intersections of crip and queer lived experience.

"μῆνῐς" ("mênis") refers to the ancient Greek word for rage or wrath, usually of a divine nature. This poem first appeared in an earlier form in Raymond Luczak's *Lovejets: Queer Male Poets on 200 Years of Walt Whitman* (Squares & Rebels, 2019). This and the subsequent poem are indebted to formative encounters with Paul Monette's *Love Alone: 18 Elegies for Rog* (St. Martin's, 1988) and Thom Gunn's *The Man With Night Sweats* (Faber & Faber, 1992).

"Advance Directive" first appeared in an earlier form in Raymond Luczak's Lovejets: *Queer Male Poets on 200 Years of Walt Whitman* (Squares & Rebels, 2019).

"Incantation for Access" begins with an epigraph drawn from Jennifer Doyle's *Campus Security*, a pamphlet produced for the Whitney Museum of Art's Biennial in 2014. The reference to the "clock that bends my body" directly references Alison Kafer's definition of "crip time" in *Feminist, Queer, Crip* (Indiana University Press, 2013): "rather than bend disabled bodies and minds to meet the clock, crip time bends the clock to meet disabled bodies and minds" (27).

"To my rib" first appeared in an earlier form in *Stone Pacific Zine's* Voice Lux Poetry Folio, Issue 9.

"Listening to Incense" first appeared in an earlier form in *Impossible Archetype* in 2018. The poem begins with a play on lines from Alfred Tennyson's "In Memoriam A. H. H" (1850).

"On Purchasing a Cane" is a golden shovel composed of a line from Alan Moore and Eddie Campbell's graphic novel, *From Hell*, published serially from 1989-1998.

"Papers, Please" is for my paternal great grandfather and his generation that made it possible for us to be here.

"Happy Valley" is for my paternal grandparents, both of whom I have never had the opportunity to meet. They are buried in St. Michael's Catholic Cemetery in Happy Valley on Hong Kong Island.

"Elegy for Security" is for my late uncle whose story remains untold.

"Funeral for Unreturned Ashes" first appeared in the Academy of American Poets' "Poem-a-Day" series in 2023 and was selected by guest editor, Steve Bellin-Oka. The poem was written in memory of my uncle who, at the time of this poem's composition, was yet to be laid to rest.

"Face Reading" first appeared in *Hypertext Magazine* in 2021 and was written in memory of my maternal grandmother. It was also nominated for the Pushcart Prize.

"Intended" first appeared in an earlier form in *Up the Staircase Quarterly* in 2016. The epigraph is a set of lines questionably attributed to Anna Akhmatova.

"What Mama Gave Me" first appeared in an earlier form in *Random Sample Review* in 2016. The epigraph is a line from Lauren Groff's *Fates and Furies* (2016).

"To my nipple" first appeared in an earlier form in a folio of poems curated by D. A. Powell for *Action, Spectacle* in 2022. Thank you, dear Jazz, for seeing me as a poet.

"Dorsality" first appeared in the "Disability Justice" issue of *The Massachusetts Review* (63.4, 2022).

"Feverish" first appeared in *ANMLY* in 2023.

"Brooded" was first drafted in Richie Hofmann's "Sensual Time: Writing the Lyric Moment in Short Poems" workshop with the Hudson Valley Writers Center in 2023. I am grateful to Richie and my fellow workshop participants for their support of this work and for helping me arrive at this little sliver of time at the heart of this poem.

"Reencountered, Months Later" first appeared in the Disability Justice issue of *The Massachusetts Review* (63.4, 2022).

"Afterglow" first appeared in Asian American Writer's Workshop's digital magazine, *The Margins* in 2024.

"Commuted" first appeared in an earlier form in *Impossible Archetype*, Issue 8 in 2020.

"Onania" draws its title from an infamous eighteenth-century medical treatise, *Onania: or, the heinous sin of self-pollution and all its frightful consequences (in both sexes) considered with spiritual and physical advice to those who have already injured themselves by this abominable practice* (H. Cooke, 1756). Its epigraph is a line from Ocean Vuong's "Ode to Masturbation" from *Night Sky with Exit Wounds* (Copper Canyon Press, 2016).

"In the dead of" first appeared in Issue Four of *fourteen poems: a queer poetry anthology* (2021). Its title is a play on Orville Peck's "Dead of Night" (*Pony*, 2019).

"Found Wanting" first appeared in *Moist Poetry Journal* in 2022.

"Cento for Wantonness" is a poem composed of lines drawn from the works of Carol Ann Duffy, Jane Hirshfield, Li-Young Lee, Carl Phillips, Richard Siken, Susan Stewart, Christian Wiman, each of whom has shaped me in more ways than I can adequately describe.

"Cobwebs: a Study" first appeared in *Apiary Magazine* in their "Essential" Issue (2020).

Acknowledgments

In the spirit of my own writing practice, which is defined by an indebtedness to the thinking and tenderness of others, I want to acknowledge that this project (really every project) is the product of interdependence. I cannot begin to properly thank everyone who made this collection possible (for even I did not fully believe I was capable of completing it), but here is my humble attempt that will inevitably be incomplete:

To my parents who have embraced my creative work from the beginning: thank you for entrusting me to tell our family's stories with boldness and with dignity.

To my godsiblings and godmother who have been more like family to me than my own blood.

To my partner, Nolan, for teaching me what tenderness means as an ongoing practice between two people who love each other. May we remain tender to one another and continue learning how to be more tender to each other. To your parents, too, for embracing me so wholeheartedly.

To my Mercury who has modeled for me that tenderness is often slowness—an intentional presentness.

To Adam Clevenger for keeping me asking the tough questions and holding space for me to struggle toward the answers.

To Doug Black and Lindsey Tomaso for keeping the pain at bay.

To Don James McLaughlin for making me realize at my own chapbook launch in Tulsa that tenderness was what this collection was really about. Thank you for helping me arrive at this title, which now feels so obviously the right one.

To my editor, Allison Blevins, who extended an open invitation to read my work years ago and believed in this collection enough to publish it. I never thought my debut collection would be taken up so soon, but I could not have asked for better crip hands in which to entrust it.

My gratitude, as well, to all the folks at Small Harbor Publishing: Kristiane Weeks-Rogers for shepherding my book through to publication, Jessica Ballen for the careful editorial eye on my manuscript, Brianna Protesto for helping bring my cover to life.

To Steve Bellin-Oka who took a risk on my work and invested in me as a poet that could inaugurate your series at Fork Tine Press. Thank you for all the opportunities you've shared with me and helping me find community.

To Kevin Wilson Kinzer whose drawings I have long admired now grace the cover of this book. Our meeting at Shipwreck Shirley's annual Luau felt like kismet: hard to believe I now get to call you a friend and a collaborator.

To my Kenyon community (past and present) who never made me choose between being a scholar or being a poet. I am so fortunate to be at an institution where my colleagues encourage me to do the work that matters most to me and to do it compassionately and sustainably:

A toast of baby wine (okay, let's face it, geriatric wine) to my department mates: Elinam Agbo, Alex Brostoff, Molly McCully Brown, Piers Brown, Frances Cannon, Jim Carson, Cristina Correa, Adele Davidson, Kathleen Fernando, Melissa Faliveno,

Kelly Fleming, Jennifer Galvão, Daimys Garcia, Andy Grace, Sarah Heidt, Michael Leong, Sergei Lobanov-Rostovsky, David Lynn, Ted Mason, Jesse Matz, Janet McAdams, Kim McMullen, Cindy Juyoung Ok, Rosemary O'Neill, Keija Parssinen, Misha Rai, Alyssa Quinn, Jené Schoenfeld, Sarah Star, Matt Suazo, Ira Sukrungruang, Brianna Thompson, and Orchid Tierney.

Beyond English, I am grateful to Robert Bennett, Hilary Buxton, Catherine Calvin, Krista Dalton, Ruthann Daniel-Harteis, Rhea Debussy, Anton Dudley, Dani Ezor, Laurie Finke, Rob Franco, Simon Garcia, Paul Gebhardt, Tom Giblin, Frankie Gourrier, Mort Guiney, Austin Johnson, Jodi Kovach, Gilda Rodriguez Wendy Singer, and Charlotte Woolf.

To my Columbus community who has welcomed me so warmly since I arrived in the thick of the pandemic. Cheers for helping me make this city my home and believing that my work deserves to be part of it: David Buehrer, Bobby Davison, Noah Demland, Terrence Dent, Brendan Downing, Mark Dunaway, Jonathan Dunkin, Trey Edmond, Marc Gofstein, Jeff Goss, Phil Hayes, Brian Humrichhouser, Scott King-Owen, Chase Kuhn, John Luna, Dee Miller, Doug Motz, Mike Nowlin, Eric Paton, Stephen Patrick, Todd Popp, Sam Risak, Robbie Schelling, Josh Stokes, Ryan Unger, Chris Vongsavath, Tim Yanok, Kevin Zimmerman.

Special shoutouts to Darren Demaree for inviting me to read alongside you at some of my very first public readings in Columbus, as well as to Dan Brewster and Gary Lovely for generously holding so much space for me at Prologue Bookshop and at Two Dollar Radio.

To the Greater Columbus Arts Council and its generous donors for the lifechanging Artists Elevated grant, which has made possible the cover art of this book and so much of the work I want to do for this next chapter of my writing practice and career.

To my Austin and UT communities for helping me find my center again after graduate school—those two precarious years profoundly transformed my work and taught me how to navigate this career. Hook 'em, longhorns: Sam Baker, J.K. Barret, Phil Barrish, Micah Bateman, Chad Bennett, Liz Cullingford, Andrew Dell'Antonio, Alan Friedman, Carrie Fountain, Jeremy Goheen, Zach Hines, Neville Hoad, Heather Houser, Martin Kevorkian, Alison Kafer, Allen MacDuffie, Julie Minich, Lisa Moore, Lisa Olstein, Sam Pinto, Elizabeth Richmond-Garza, Liz Scala, Ana Schwartz, Weston Richey, and Jorie Woods.

To my dear colleagues who have cared for me from afar and believed in my work when I did not, who have held space for my work in your classrooms and in your own writing—here's to a department without walls, to quote *Synapsis: A Journal of Health Humanities Journal*'s mission: Cass Adair, Michael Allan, Sari Altschuler, Kat Alves, Remy Attig, Ben Baker, Steph Ban, Emily Beitiks, Ayendy Bonifacio, Saronik Bosu, Manu Chander, Andrea Charise, Cate Belling, Kaitlin Blanchard, Fiona Brideoake, Gracen Brilmyer, Chase Bringardner, Lydia Brown, Shalyn Claggett, Alberto Carbajal, John Carranza, Seo-Young Chu, Noah Chaskin, Tita Chico, Lauren Eriks Cline, Pierre Cloutier de Repentigny, Matthew Cortland, Louise Creechan, Sarah Currie, Mint Damrongpiwat, Jenny Davidson, Carolyn Day, Cate Denial, Kathryn Desplanque, Helen Deutsch, Amrita Dhar, Jay Dolmage, Douglas Dowland, Joe Drury, Zoë Eckman, Nirmala Erevelles, Jason Farr, Ryan Fong, Elaine Freedgood, Dustin Friedman, Emily Friedman, Julia Ftacek, Stephen Furlong, D. Chris Gabbard, Michael Gamer, Devin Garofalo, Mike Gill, Corey Goergen, Catherine Goldstead, Caroline Gonda, Roger Grant, Devin Griffiths, John Gulledge, Soren

Hammerschmidt, Ashley Shew Heflin, Nic Helms, Carolyn Hembree, Stephanie Hershinow, Kwame Holmes, Sandy Ho, Fintan Hoey, Martha Stoddard Holmes, Margie Housley, Ada Hubrig, Neil Hultgren, Amy Huseby, Vox Jo Hsu, Jonathan Hsy, Damien Huffer, Annie Hwang, Cody Jackson, Matthew Johnson, Merri Lisa Johnson, Olivera Jokić, L. Bellee Jones-Pierce, Roanne Kantor, Declan Kavanagh, Paul Kelleher, Andy Kesson, Joey Kim, Matthew Kim, Kit Kincade, Ula Klein, Scott Gabriel Knowles, Danny Kodmur, Misty Krueger, Mimi Khúc, Emily Kugler, Heather Ann Ladd, Greta LaFleur, Sue Lanser, Alexander Lester, Jacob Leveton, Daniel Libatique, Chris Loar, Nicole Lobdell, John Loeppky, Thomas Long, Devoney Looser, Ashley Lu, Kathy Lubey, Timothy Lyle, Vyshali Manivannan, Maddy Mant, Alan Martino, Tricia Matthew, Harry McCarthy, Elaine McGirr, Robert McRuer, Neko Mellor, Omar Miranda, Heather Mitchell-Buck, Apara Nair, Mona Narain, Adam Newman, Trung Nguyen, Sal Nicolazzo, Marissa Nicosia, Emilia Nielsen, Kari Nixon, Kate Ozment, Andew Pegoda, Megan Peiser, Chelsea Phillips, Matthew Phillips, Ben Pladek, Margaret Price, Jake Pyne, Bethany Qualls, Manasvin Rajagopalan, Grace Rexroth, Matthew Reznicek, Jared Richman, Julia Miele Rodas, Gabriel Rosenberg, Helen Rottier, Ellen Samuels, Kirsten Saxton, Talia Schaffer, Nicole Lee Schroeder, Lorenzo Servitje, Carrie Shanafelt, Emma Sheppard, Bassam Sidiki, Marisa Siegel, Logan Smilges, Sharon Snyder, Erin Spampinato, Emily Stanback, Jordan Stein, Laura Stevens, Tyler Tennant, Milan Terlunen, Courtney Thompson, Jean-Thomas Tremblay, David Turner, Anwar Uhuru, Jamie Utphall, CJ Valasek, Maggie Vanderford, Erik Wade, Miriam Wallace, Emily Waples, Chris Washington, Sara Wasson, Geoff Way, Jason Weidemann, Jordan Welsh, Eric Weinstein, Jarred Wiehe, Diane Wiener, Claude Willan, Xine Yao, Sam Yates, Gena Zuroski.

To Aaron Gorelik who first introduced me to the HIV/AIDS-era poets and made me learn my queer history. Thank you for everything you've taught me—my work began with our work together.

To my students (past, present, and future): you continue to sustain me and remind me why this is all worth doing.

To my fellow writers and artists who remind me to/for whom I write and what the stakes *really are*: Tory Adkisson, Phoenix Alexander, Ashna Ali, Denise Nicole Andrews, Cindy Arrieu-King, Ruth Awad, Kay Ulanday Barrett, Jason Bartles, Oliver Baez Bendorf, Rosebud Ben-Oni, Jay Besemer, Kayla Besse, Sheila Black, Julia Bloch, Daniel Brenchi-Sluman, Bryan Borland, Dustin Brookshire, Rachel Bunting, Jake Byrne, Grace Caggiano, Chris Campanioni, Robert Carr, Charlie Carter, Noelia Cerna, Alexander Chee, Chen Chen, Marlena Chertok, Ava Anne Cipri, Emily Rose Cole, Rob Colgate, John Compton, Adam Day, Meg Day, Jim Ferris, Jamie Andersen Fields, Kenny Fries, Catie Garbinsky, Tea Gerbeza, Marcos Gonsalez, torrin greathouse, David Groff, Andrew Gurza, Roy Guzmán, Alex Haagard, Zane Hagans, Raye Hendrix, Chris Herrmann, Richie Hofmann, Amanda Hollander, Rob Jacques, Charles Jensen, Cyrée Jarelle Johnson, Luke Johnson, Camisha Jones, Bellee Jones-Pierce, Ilya Kaminsky, Randy Kim, Frances Klein, Ben Kline, Julia Kolchinsky-Dasbach, Steve Kuusisto, Susan Leary, Daniel Lee, Nania Lee, Zach Linge, Chris Lloyd, Lucia Lorenzi, Raymond Luczak, Liv Mammone, Rita Maria Martinez, Toby Mayer, John McCullough, Kristina McMullin, Sarah Montgomery, Ellie Musgrave, Joe Nasta, Patrick Nathan, Mike Northen, Naomi Ortiz, Brody Parrish, Seth Pennington, Carl Phillips, Leah Lakshmi Piepzna-Samarasinha, Maya Popa, Justin Porter, D.A. Powell, Jason Purcell, Ruben Quesada, Ricky Ray, Jesse Rice-Evans, Jordy Rosenberg, C.T. Salazar, Scott Senko, Sejal Shah, Jane Shi, Coyote Shook, Ross Showalter, Danez Smith, Hayden Smith, Jessica Smith, Jen Soriano, Nathan Spoon, Dan Stephensen, Den Sweeney, Ben Townley-Canning, Eric Tran, Val

Vera, Addie Tsai, Viktoria Valenzuela, Donna Vorreyer, Mathew Yates, C. Dale Young, Sara Wagner, Susie Walsh, Mark Ward, Jillian Weise, Jim Whiteside, Alice Wong, Scott Woods, Brendon Zatirka, Su Zi.

To Yumi Sakugawa whose workshops and meditative practice helped me reconnect with my writing practice.

To my friends who have never let space and time keep us from caring for one another, who have witnessed me from afar: Rob Connoley, Derek Finn, Peter Frolio, Victoria Gao, Tara Goldberg, Christopher Jack, Josh Jagerman, Andrew Jones, Doug Kikuta, Kinan Lagast, Mike Madaio, Matt McWilliams, Thanasis Platis, Keegan Shepherd, Matt Shiverdecker, Therese Stephen, Jim Tran.

Often, "the work of living"—especially the work of minoritized living —is the work of coming to understand how we have been shaped by violent, tender inheritances and laboring, slowly, to become our own shapes. In this tradition, Travis Chi Wing Lau's *What's Left Is Tender* is a virtuosic act of crip/queer/ diasporic formalism. The poems curve and fracture and hobble and speak across their own gaps; they work with and against received poetic forms; they take up unexpected postures on the page. And, through this careful attention to form, Lau is able to attend with as much care to the tender knots of queer shame and desire, family inheritance as debt and condition of possibly, medicine as violence and promise of relief. In this way, line by line, Lau carries his reader through a "quiet manifesto" on what it takes to truly honor and be directed by the queer, crip, and otherwise "deviant will // that shapes our form," on the futures available to us if we attend, with each other, to their "soft making."

   —Cameron Awkward Rich, author of *Sympathetic Little Monster* (Ricochet Editions, 2016), *Transit* (Button Poetry, 2017), *Dispatch: poems* (Persea Books, 2019), and *The Terrible We: Thinking With Trans Maladjustment* (Duke University Press, 2022)

From list to radical erasure, from abecedarian to wailing prayer and "quiet manifestos," this formally restless book challenges a world bent on stamping out bodies deemed error and desires named aberrant, not worth the music that pulses on every page here. No, these poems say, pay attention, "dream of that nectar again." Travis Chi Wing Lau is that rare poet who can combine deep erudition with keen feeling—his literary and historical references are many and layered, but never does he lose his capacity for concrete intimacy, for addressing, say his own nipple. "May you mackerel / with majesty," declares another poem, and I believe that I will do just that, for I am swayed by its sound—and by, yes, the tenderness.

   —Chen Chen, author of *When I Grow Up I Want to Be a List of Further Possibilities* (BOA Editions, 2017) and *Your Emergency Contact Has Experienced an Emergency* (BOA Editions, 2022)

Shuttling dynamically between the languages of myth and medicine, drawing on inheritances from family and from literary history, *What's Left Is Tender* investigates the body's fragility—its bewildering, alluring hardness and softness. The poems themselves make dazzling shapes on the page and in the mind. In Travis Chi Wing Lau's deeply learned and deeply felt poems, "full of / your tender / zeal," we find a craft for living.

> —Richie Hofmann, author of *Second Empire* (Alice James, 2015) and *A Hundred Lovers* (Alfred A. Knopf, 2022)

Very rarely one opens a debut poetry collections and feels one is reading the author's fifth or sixth book--it is *that* captivating, and skillful. Travis Chi Wing Lau's *What's Left Is Tender* is such a book. But why? Because the metaphysics of the body here are given a myriad perspectives, from the author's own story, to travail of the horrorshow known as contemporary American medical system, to the larger question of what it means, after all, to be alive in the body, to the *very* lovely sensual lyrics teaching us that "compassion is a holding" — this book is bursting with possibilities of "body and its discontents". Then, there is the question of Lau's treatment of English language, which, to my mind, is disability poetics at its best: formal inventiveness here happens not because the author is showing off their obviously considerable knowledge various formal skills, but because it is viscerally, humanly necessary: there is no other way to say a thing except via innovation. Indeed, reading this book one can see what Mallarme meant when he said that poem is not about an event, it *is* an event, which is to say: here's a poetics that invents an elegance all its own, "a tendering". Beautiful, necessary work.

> —Ilya Kaminsky, author of *Dancing in Odessa* (Tupelo Press, 2004) and *Deaf Republic* (Graywolf Press, 2019)

Travis Chi Wing Lau's *What's Left is Tender* reveals discoveries like a mosaic. The poles and magnetic fields of internal crippledness are illuminated on the wall. These poems are by turns ironic, bold, and affectionate.

—Stephen Kuusisto, author of *Planet of the Blind* (Dial Press, 1998), *Only Bread, Only Light* (Copper Canyon Press, 2000), *Eavesdropping: A Memoir of Blindness and Listening* (W. W. Norton, 2006), and *Letters to Borges* (Copper Canyon Press, 2013)

Travis Chi Wing Lau's dexterity of form reminds us that one is both broken by and healed by poetry: it keeps vivid account of what is felt by our massive nervous system as we encounter the pains of living inside our bodies. It also provides a way to cast spells, to invoke powers beyond our limitations and to harness that energy for our renewal and restoration. These poems are architectural wonders, intricate as spider webs and with that same tensile strength that defies any attempt to break its liquid surface. They are seismic eruptions recorded with a sensitive needle, the transcriptions of what shook and moved the ground beneath the poet's feet. You, too, reader, feel the tremorous effect of these tremendous terrestrial events.

—D. A. Powell, author of *Chronic: Poems* (Graywolf Press, 2009), *Useless Landscape, or a Guide for Boys: Poems* (Graywolf Press, 2012), *Repast: Tea, Lunch, Cocktails* (Graywolf Press, 2014)

At no point does Travis Chi Wing Lau let you forget that the soul resides within a body, regardless of how that body is seen. In *What's Left is Tender*, Lau asks us to consider what it means to be tender, not as a result of violent hammering but as a result of tenderness begetting tenderness. In poems that refuse to avert their gaze, Lau requests we reconsider the body. "Be prepared for your flesh and your name, like your days, to be numbered," he writes. Be prepared for this collection to take hold of you and not let go.

—C. Dale Young, author of *The Day Underneath the Day* (TriQuarterly Books, 2001), *The Second Person* (Four Way Books, 2007), *Torn* (Four Way Books, 2011), *The Halo* (Four Way Books, 2016), *Prometeo* (Four Way Books, 2021), and *Building the Perfect Animal: New and Selected Poems* (Four Way Books, 2025)

Travis Chi Wing Lau (he/him/his) is the author of three previous chapbook collections: *The Bone Setter* (Damaged Goods Press, 2019), *Paring* (Finishing Line Press, 2020), and *Vagaries* (Fork Tine Press, 2022). His poetry has appeared or is forthcoming in The Academy of American Poets' "Poem-A-Day" series, The Asian American Writers' Workshop's *The Margins* series, *Action, Spectacle, Barren Magazine, Cincinnati Review, fourteen poems, Foglifter, Glass, Hypertext, Impossible Archetype, Nat. Brut, Rogue Agent, The South Carolina Review, Tupelo Quarterly* among many others. His work has been nominated for both the Pushcart Prize and *Best of the Net* Anthology, republished in *Queer Nature* (Autumn House Press, 2022), and longlisted in the *Best American Essays* anthology (2020). He was the winner of the Christopher Hewitt Award for Poetry (2019) and a recipient of the Greater Columbus Arts Council's Artists Elevated Prize (2024). He is co-editor of *Every Place on the Map Is Disabled: Poems and Essays on Disability* (Northwestern University Press, 2026). He holds a B.A. in English/Classics from UCLA, M.A. & Ph.D. in English from The University of Pennsylvania. He currently teaches eighteenth and nineteenth-century British literature and culture, health humanities, and disability studies at Kenyon College and lives in Columbus, Ohio.

About Small Harbor Publishing

Small Harbor Publishing is a 501c3 nonprofit organization. Our goal is to publish unique and diverse voices. We are a feminist press, and we are committed to diversity and inclusion. We strive to bring new voices to a devoted and expanding readership.

Small Harbor Publishing began in 2018 with the first issue of *Harbor Review*. The magazine is an online space where poetry and art converse. *Harbor Review* quickly grew and now publishes reviews and runs multiple micro chapbook competitions, including the Washburn Prize and the Editor's Prize.

In July 2020, Small Harbor Publishing was officially incorporated and began Harbor Editions. Harbor Editions accepts submissions through a chapbook open reading period, a hybrid chapbook open reading period, the Marginalia Series, and the Laureate Prize.

In 2023, Harbor Anthologies began with a mission to promote texts that explore social justice issues and highlight marginalized writers.

If you would like to support Small Harbor Publishing, visit our "About" page at: smallharborpublishing.com/about.